VELOCIRAPTOR: SMALL AND SPEEDY

by Dawn Bentley
Illustrated by Karen Carr

SMITHSONIAN INSTITUTION

For Nile Alexander. Love, Aunt Dawn. — D.B.

Dedicated with love and appreciation to Dr. Bonnie F. Jacobs of the Environmental Science Program at SMU, whose work educates and enlightens. — K.C.

Book copyright © 2003 Trudy Corporation
and the Smithsonian Institution, Washington DC 20560

Published by Soundprints Division of Trudy Corporation, Norwalk, Connecticut.

Book design: Marcin D. Pilchowski
Editor: Laura Gates Galvin
Editorial assistance: Chelsea Shriver

First Edition 2003
10 9 8 7 6 5 4 3 2 1
Printed in China

Acknowledgements:
    Our very special thanks to Dr. Brett-Surman of the Smithsonian Institution's National Museum of Natural History.
    Soundprints would like to thank Ellen Nanney and Katie Mann of the Smithsonian Institution for their help in the creation of the book.

Library of Congress Cataloging-in-Publication Data

Bentley, Dawn
    Veociraptor : small and speedy / by Dawn Bentley ; illustrated by Karen Carr.
 p. cm.
Summary: When a velociraptor and his pack explore a valley for food, water, and new challenges, the other animals get out of their way.
  ISBN 1-59249-161-8 (HC) – ISBN 1-59249-162-6 (pbk.) – ISBN 1-59249-163-4 (micro)
 [1. Velociraptor—Fiction. 2. Dinosaurs—Fiction.] I. Carr, Karen, 1960- ill. II. Title

PZ7.B447494Ve 2003
 [E]—dc21

                                                                    2003050359

VELOCIRAPTOR: SMALL AND SPEEDY

by Dawn Bentley

Illustrated by Karen Carr

Soundprints

Where Children Discover...

The sun beats down on the dry, hot land. A hand with long fingers and sharp claws creeps over the edge of the rocky hill. Another hand follows. Then a head peeks up and two eyes look back and forth at the valley below.

In a sudden burst, the creature jumps to the top of the ridge for a better view. It's a Velociraptor! The 50-pound, bird-like dinosaur stands on his two legs. Even though he is only three feet tall, Velociraptor does not have much to fear. He is smart, fast and fierce!

Velociraptor sees what he's been looking for — the other Velociraptors in his pack. He runs down the hill to join them. Together they will explore the area looking for food.

Velociraptor is in the lead as they race over the hot dirt. He runs as fast as he can. His stiff tail sticks straight out, helping him stay balanced so he can make quick turns. He is one of the fastest runners in all the land!

Velociraptor sees a Gallimimus far in the distance. The Gallimimus is much bigger and runs just as fast as Velociraptor. But Velociraptor is very smart. It doesn't take him long to figure out a way he and the other Velociraptors can catch the Gallimimus.

The Velociraptors separate, each going their own way. The Gallimimus doesn't notice they are there until it's too late. The Velociraptors lunge at the dinosaur from every direction, tackling him to the ground. With dozens of sharp claws aiming at him, the Gallimimus can't fight them off.

Velociraptor is always on the lookout for more food. Soon, he sees an Oviraptor feasting on a nest of eggs. The Oviraptor is lucky she sees the pack coming! She quickly runs away. Velociraptor and his pack eat the eggs, then speed off to see what else they can find.

In a small stream nearby, animals gather to drink. There is not much water in the dry valley, so many animals must share what little there is. As Velociraptor and his pack run to the water, all the creatures scatter, leaving the area as fast as they can!

Velociraptor hears howling in the distance. A Protoceratops and an Oviraptor are fighting. Velociraptor and his group rush toward them to get a better look, but as they get closer the dinosaurs run away. No one wants to fight when there's a pack of Velociraptors around!

Velociraptor is tired. He lies down to rest. He flicks out the three-inch claw on his middle toe to clean it. He must take good care of his claws—they are his most powerful tools.

A little mammal scurries by, hoping to get to the safety of a crevice just a few feet away. With a swipe of his claws, Velociraptor traps him. He moves his wrists up and down to catch the animal. Velociraptor isn't hungry, but he never misses the chance to practice his hunting skills.

Soon, Velociraptor hears the sound of pounding steps in the distance. Velociraptor is always ready for action! He and the other Velociraptors leap to their feet and head toward the thumping steps, excited to find out what new challenge awaits them!

ABOUT THE VELOCIRAPTOR
(vee-LOSS-ee-RAP-tor)

Velociraptors lived during the Late Cretaceous Period, about 75 million years ago. They weighed up to 50 pounds and were about three feet tall. That is probably smaller than you are. They were much smaller than the bigger dinosaurs that lived during that time.

Velociraptors had big brains and were very smart. They could run up to 25 miles per hour and change directions very quickly by swinging their tails. That means they were probably able to catch almost any dinosaur they chased.